50 GREAT OBJECT LESSONS THAT BRING THE BIBLE TO LIFE

All Rights Reserved
Mark J Musser Books
2015

Special Thanks To:
God for guiding my steps
and for my wife and son who put up with my missteps

Scriptures cited are from: *Holy Bible. New Living Translation copyright© 1996, 2004, 2007, 2013 by Tyndale House Foundation. Used by permission of Tyndale House Publishers Inc., Carol Stream, Illinois 60188.* All rights reserved.

PARENTING BOOKS BY MARK J MUSSER

Lessons on Parenting:
What Parents in the Bible Can Teach Parents Today

The Bible is full of insightful and meaningful narratives where Moms and Dads are found making choices that impact their children and those around them. The blessings or fallout from those choices and decisions most definitely can apply to our lives as parents today.

The Christ Centered Home:
Turning Your Kids into Christ-Centered Disciples

Long before God established the nation of Israel to be His chosen people, and long before He established the church to spread His glory, He established the family to be the primary means of making disciples. Is your family fulfilling that mandate?

Parenting Essentials:
Ten Things Every Parent Should Do

Do you know what you should be doing as a Christian parent? Do you understand what essential characteristics must be modeled for your children and teens? These are the questions this family-defining book seeks to answer.

Soul Sick
The Causes of Spiritual Disease in Our Children

As surely as the young are most susceptible to physical disease, so it is with diseases of the soul. What are these diseases that seek after our children's souls? How can we guard against them? Answering those questions is the purpose of this generation defining book

30 DAY FAMILY DEVOTIONALS

TABLE TALKS
Discovering Who God Really Is

TABLE TALKS
Making a Difference for Jesus

TABLE TALKS
What it Means to be A Christian

TABLE TALKS
Christmas is Jesus' Birthday, Not Yours

Check out these titles,
and find free resources, at www.markjmusser.com

TABLE OF OBJECT LESSONS

A Clean Heart	--	Isaiah 1:18
Filled with God	--	Isaiah 55:8-9
Ready to Listen	--	Mark 4:23-25
Shine Out	--	Matthew 5:14-16
Getting Wisdom…	--	James 1:15
Always Ready to Listen	--	Deuteronomy 13:4
The Power of God's Love	--	Jeremiah 31:1-3
Be Led by Someone Greater	--	Isaiah 45:11-12
Patience is a Virtue	--	Jeremiah 29:10-11
Are You in God's Will?	--	Rom. 8:28; Rev. 3:15-16
Letting God Take Control	--	1 Peter 1:14-16
The Right Focus	--	Matthew 6:21-24
We Need Each Other	--	Romans 12:5
Show & Tell	--	1 John 3:16-18
All Things Are Possible	--	Mark 10:27
A Fitness Regimen	--	1 Timothy 4:7-12
Finish the Race	--	2 Timothy 4:5-8
Time for a Test	--	1 Peter 1:7
Attitude and Obedience	--	John 14:23-24
Releasing the Burden	--	1 Peter 5:7
Life's Map	--	Proverbs 2:1-5
Got Wisdom?	--	Proverbs 3:5-7
Get Plugged In	--	Ephesians 3:19-20
Walk the Talk	--	Luke 6:46-49
What Would You Do If…	--	1 Cor. 11:1; Eph. 5:1-2
Mirrors of Christ	--	Philippians 3:17-20
Ready to Overflow	--	Psalm 63:1-5
God's Kingdom First…	--	Matthew 6:31-33
Controlled by Love	--	John 13:34-35
Time to Transform	--	2 Corinthians 5:15
Letting God Take Over	--	Galatians 2:19-20
Fruit Inspection	--	Matthew 7:15-20
Whatcha Thinkin' About?	--	Colossians 3:1-4

Get Connected	--	John 15:1-8
Washed Clean	--	1 John 1:8-9
Being Made New	--	1 Timothy 1:14-16
Kingdom Heirs	--	Galatians 4:4-7
Time in the Word	--	2 Timothy 3:16-17
Treasure Seeker	--	Matthew 13:44-46
Alien Invasion	--	1 Peter 2:11-12
Stick Out in a Crowd	--	Philippians 1:27
Stop the Confusion	--	Ezekiel 36:20-22
Hey, What's that Smell?	--	2 Corinthians 2:14-15
Dull or Bright?	--	2 Corinthians 3:7-9
Stuck in the Soil	--	1 John 2:24-25
Always Best to Obey	--	John 14:15
Multiplying the Kingdom	--	Romans 10:13-15
The Rub Off	--	1 Corinthians 15:33
Changing Your Mind	--	Philippians 2:4-5
Picked Back Up	--	Psalm 147:1-3

Epilogue

A CLEAN HEART
Isaiah 1:18

THE POINT
Sin, left unchecked, always spreads and causes all sorts of problems in our lives. Yet, because of Jesus' sacrifice, we can stop sin's spread and be made new!

THE PREP
About five minutes to gather a few items

THE PROPS
A clear glass; water; dark food coloring

THE PROCESS
- Get out a clear glass and fill it with water. Gather the kids around and put one single drop of food coloring into the glass
- As you all watch the single drop spread through the water, talk about how unchecked sin spreads in our hearts, causing all sorts of problems
- After sharing this truth, pour out the glass and refill it with fresh water
- Discuss how the Bible says God gives us new, clean hearts when we accept Jesus and seek forgiveness for our sins

FILLED WITH GOD
Isaiah 55:8 & 9

THE POINT
God is greater, mightier, bigger, and smarter than we can ever imagine. We can never fully understand Him, yet we should always seek to be filled with as much of Him as we can.

THE PREP
About five minutes to gather a few items

THE PROPS
A small cup, like a tea-cup; a bucket; water; dark-colored liquid

THE PROCESS—PART 1
- Get an empty tea cup and fill a bucket with water. Pour the water from the bucket into the tea cup
- Explain how God is like the bucket and we are like the tea cup.
- We can never fully understand God, but we should spend our lives trying to be as filled with Him as possible

THE PROCESS—PART 2
- Empty the tea cup and refill the bucket with water
- Now fill the tea-cup half way with dark soda or another dark-colored liquid
- Repeat that God is like the bucket and we are like the tea cup. We need to be filled with God's wisdom and love; however, to do so, we need to be empty of ourselves
- Pour some water from the bucket into the tea-cup and show the family how water is mixed with the dark liquid
- Explain that God cannot fill us with His good things until all our things are gone
- Pour more water from the bucket into the tea-cup until all the dark-liquid is gone
- Discuss what sins, wrong ideas, bad habits, etc. might be filling each of

you
- Pray and ask God to remove those things, so that you can be filled to the brim with Him

READY TO LISTEN
Mark 4:23-25

THE POINT
God is always seeking to speak to us. He wants to guide us and lead us. However, we often do not hear Him simply because we seldom take the time to listen.

THE PREP
None

THE PROPS
None

THE PROCESS
- Ask your kids to try to explain something fun that happened today *without* talking
- After their attempts, ask, "Did you find that it was frustrating to share what happened without using words?"
- Explain that this is how God feels sometimes. He wants to speak to us, to explain things to us, but He can't if we don't take the time to listen in prayer
- Make a plan to pray with your family at dinner, or before bed, every night

SHINE OUT!
Matthew 5:14-16

THE POINT
We are called to shine brightly for Christ. Our lives should be bright neon signs that point people to Jesus.

THE PREP
A couple minutes to gather two items

THE PROPS
At least one flashlight; a hand-held mirror

THE PROCESS—PART 1
- Take a flashlight and shine it right into your children's faces
- Talk about how everyone knows when a bright light shines in their face
- Similarly, shining for God means everyone should know that we love Him and follow Him. It should be obvious by our words, our actions, and our attitudes
- Discuss ways that your family can shine for Jesus

THE PROCESS-PART 2
- Hold the hand-held mirror out in front of you and shine the flashlight in the mirror so that the light reflects back at you
- Discuss how we can either use what God has given us to make ourselves look good and give ourselves glory or to make Him look good and give Him glory
- Next, angle the mirror so that the light reflects off of it and shines on the children
- Finish by reviewing how well your family is reflecting God's love to others

GETTING WISDOM WHEN YOU NEED IT
James 1:5

THE POINT
God has all the wisdom we need. He knows everything—including the future. We don't need to try to guess our way through life, hoping to make the right choices. All we need to do is ask God.

THE PREP
Minimal

THE PROPS
A deck of cards

THE PROCESS
- Pull out the deck of cards. Holding the cards face down, let the kids each pick one
- Take the cards so that only you can see them. Have the kids make a couple guesses
- When they have guessed wrong a few times, tell them that they can ask you for some clues
- Afterwards discuss how much easier it was when you helped them
- Talk about how much easier it is to ask God what we should do instead of trying to guess for ourselves

ALWAYS READY TO LISTEN
Deuteronomy 13:4

THE POINT
When we cannot hear the Lord or feel His presence, it is not because He has moved. It is because we have. Sadly, in the process of distancing ourselves from the Lord, we miss out on all the great things He has for us.

THE PREP
A couple minutes to find a favored snack

THE PROPS
A favorite family snack for everyone

THE PROCESS
- Gather the kids and tell them you are going to play a game of hide-n-seek. They are the hiders and you are the seeker
- After they go and hide, make yourself a bowl of ice-cream or some other favorite snack, gently whisper that you have a snack for them too. (Make sure they cannot hear you)
- Do *not* look for the kids. When the kids come out and start complaining because they've found you eating a snack instead of playing the game, tell them that you did ask if they wanted anything but they must not have heard you
- Then discuss, over a snack, that when we move ourselves from God, we make it difficult to hear Him speaking to our hearts
- Talk about ways your family can stay close to the Lord

THE POWER OF GOD'S LOVE
Jeremiah 31:1-3

THE POINT
There is no greater force in the universe than God's love. It has the amazing power to touch hearts, heal relationships, change lives, and alter eternities. Experiencing that love, and then sharing it with others, should be the focus of our lives.

THE PREP
A couple minutes to gather supplies

THE PROPS
Several pennies; refrigerator magnet(s), or other type of magnet(s), which can pull pennies across a flat surface

THE PROCESS
- With your magnet, show the kids how you can pull pennies across the kitchen table or counter top
- Talk about how God's love is much like the magnet
- It is so great that it draws people to Him
- Moreover, once we have experienced God's love, we need to turn around and help draw others to God
- Hand your children magnets and allow them to pull pennies
- Discuss ways your family can show God's love to others

BE LED BY SOMEONE GREATER
Isaiah 45:11 & 12

THE POINT
Life is difficult, especially for children. There is much in our culture that can lead them astray and cause them physical and/or spiritual harm. As older and wiser stewards of our children, we must be careful to guide them safely through life, while also pointing them to the One who guides us.

THE PREP
Ten minutes to prepare some papers

THE PROPS
An open space in your home; several pieces of paper to write on; *Sharpie* or marker; blindfold

THE PROCESS
- Place several pieces of paper on the floor with big, bold words on them like "danger," "anger," "sin," "hurt," "pain," "bad TV shows," "bullies," etc.
- After you have shown your children these papers strewn on the floor, put a blindfold on one and see if he or she can make it from one side of the room to the other without stepping on any
- Offer NO assistance
- After your children have tried unsuccessfully to make it across, tell them to walk slowly as you guide them through the papers step by step
- When safely to the other side, remove the blindfold and explain how both God and you know more than they do. It is your job to guide them through life, and it is their job to listen and follow. When they do, life goes a lot better!
- Discuss also how everyone, child and adult, needs to constantly lean on God's guidance

PATIENCE IS A VIRTUE
Jeremiah 29:10 & 11

THE POINT
God has a great plan and purpose for everyone. However, His plans and purposes are not revealed as quickly and easily as we would like. Often, we must patiently wait for the Lord's plans and purposes to unfold.

THE PREP
A couple minutes

THE PROPS
A story to tell

THE PROCESS
- Act all excited and tell your kids that you have the greatest story in the world to share with them
- When they are gathered around, begin telling them a story but share it as *slowly* as possible
- When your kids are visibly annoyed (and perhaps verbally annoyed as well!), talk about how we like things to happen quickly, but God rarely works that way
- Sometimes things, like great stories, take time. We have to be patient and wait
- Discuss areas where your family lacks patience

ARE YOU IN GOD'S WILL?
Romans 8:28; Revelation 3:15 & 16

THE POINT
The best place to be is in the center of God's will. When there, we can experience the fullness of what God has for us. Outside of His will, our lives are never quite as they should be.

THE PREP
A couple minutes

THE PROPS
Lukewarm water for everyone

THE PROCESS
- Provide glasses of lukewarm water for everyone to have while eating dinner
- When the kids complain about the taste, ask what's wrong
- Explain that the drink was not *in* the fridge, so it doesn't taste its best
- Go on to explain that if we want to experience God's best, we need to be *in* His will, seeking to do what He says
- Outside of God's will, we will never be at our best
- Discuss ways your family can make sure to stay in the center of God's will

LETTING GOD TAKE CONTROL
1 Peter 1:14-16

THE POINT
The only way to live the great life God has for us is to allow Him to take control. When the Lord is overseeing our lives, amazing things can happen. We can do things, and become things, we never thought possible!

THE PREP
None

THE PROPS
A remote control vehicle or a multi-player video game

THE PROCESS
- Play a video game with your child (or play with a remote control vehicle together)
- Discuss how the person using the controller is guiding the character on the screen (or the vehicle). A good player will do well at guiding a character (or vehicle) to do the best job possible, get the highest score, etc.
- Go on to talk about how God is *The Most Good* in the whole universe. Because of this, He can best guide our lives to the best things possible. We just need to let Him have control
- Finish by discussing areas in your lives that might not be under God's control yet

THE RIGHT FOCUS
Matthew 6:21-24

THE POINT
No one can focus on two things at the same time. Therefore, it is impossible to be focused on God and self, or God and worldly pursuits, at the same time. One will give way to the other. With that in mind, we all need to evaluate where the bulk of our focus is.

THE PREP
A couple minutes to choose two pictures

THE PROPS
Two pictures

THE PROCESS
- Have one person stand in front of a child holding up one of the pictures and one person standing behind the same child doing likewise with the other picture
- Have your child try to look at both pictures at the same time and explain what each contains
- Once it proves impossible, discuss how your child could only focus on one picture at a time. To focus on one, he or she would need to stop focusing on the other
- Talk about our need to take time out of each day to purposely stop focusing on the stuff all around us and to start focusing on God—with prayer, Bible study, devotions, etc.
- Finish by coming up with a family plan that will help you all spend more time focused on God and His Kingdom each day

WE NEED EACH OTHER
Romans 12:5

THE POINT
In our individualist society, it is important to remind ourselves that God did not create us to be independent. He created us to need Him *and* to need others.

THE PREP
A couple minutes to collect some articles of clothing and other items

THE PROPS
A button-down shirt; shoes with laces; peanut butter; bread; knife

THE PROCESS
- Hand the kids button-down shirts and shoes with the laces untied
- Tell them to put on the shirt and button it up with only one hand. Further, instruct them to put on the shoes and tie them with just one hand
- Besides having your children try to button a shirt or tie shoes with one hand, you can also see if they can spread peanut butter on a piece of bread with one hand
- After each experience, discuss how our body needs to work together to make things happen
- Talk about how the Bible says the church is like a body, and we all need to work together. We cannot "go it alone" in life

SHOW AND TELL
1 John 3:16-18

THE POINT
It is easy to say, "I am a Christian." It is not always so easy, however, to show it! Yet, it is vitally important that we *show* our Christianity. Because, in the end, people will remember our actions long after they have forgotten our words.

THE PREP
A couple minutes to prepare for charades

THE PROPS
Cards with people, things, places, written on them for the kids to act out

THE PROCESS
- Play a game of charades with the kids, giving each child a chance to act out a couple different people, places, and/or things
- Afterwards, discuss how, in charades, you have to *show* people, without using words, what is written on your card. Likewise, as Christians, we have to *show* people we are Christians by our actions and attitudes.
- Talk about what Christian actions and attitudes look like
- Finish by chatting about how your family is doing at having your actions and attitudes match the words "I am a Christian."

ALL THINGS ARE POSSIBLE
Mark 10:27

THE POINT
Life is hard. Much confronts us each day that seems impossible to deal with. Yet, with God, all things are possible. The question is, "Am I relying on Him, or am I trying to do everything myself?"

THE PREP
None

THE PROPS
None

THE PROCESS
- Give your children an impossible task—like getting to the top of the steps without touching any of the stairs (or without using their legs)
- When it proves impossible for them, offer to carry them to the top. (This way, *they* are still not touching the stairs or using their legs)
- Discuss how life often seems difficult, and there are times in life when situations seem impossible. Yet, we are never alone. God, with His strength, is always there
- Talk about how your family can rely on God through all the difficult circumstances
- Finish with prayer, asking God to carrying you through the tough times

A FITNESS REGIMEN
1 Timothy 4:7-12

THE POINT
Just as physical fitness is important to a person's physical health, so spiritual fitness is important to a person's spiritual health.

THE PREP
A few minutes to create a place to freely exercise

THE PROPS
None. Some workout equipment such as light weights, jump ropes, etc. are optional.

THE PROCESS
- Take your family through an exercise regimen
- Have them do some push-ups, jumping jacks, sit-ups, run in place, etc.
- Discuss how exercise is hard work, but it definitely helps our bodies be better, stronger, and fitter
- From there, talk about how reading the Bible, doing devotions, praying, and more can also be hard work, but it definitely helps our relationship with the Lord be better and stronger
- Finish by coming up with ways your family can *daily* focus on being physically and spiritually fit

FINISH THE RACE
2 Timothy 4:5-8

THE POINT
We are often taught that finishing first makes someone a winner. In the Christian life, however, that is not necessarily the case. It is much more important to finish *right* than to finish *first*.

THE PREP
A few minutes to gather supplies and create a "play space"

THE PROPS
A space to race; cotton balls or ping pong balls; spoons; finish line

THE PROCESS
- Clear a space for the kids to have a race
- Have them run from a starting place to a finish line. The first person to the finish line wins
- Set up a second race for the kids. This time place a cotton ball, or ping pong ball, on a spoon that each child will hold in his or her dominant hand
- The first person to get from start to finish without the cotton ball, or ping pong ball, falling off the spoon is the winner
- Discuss how the Christian life is much more like the second race than the first
- As Christians, we have to take careful steps to make sure that we successfully get to the end of each day having honored God in all we said, thought, and did
- Finish by discussing any weak areas in each family member. Chat about how proceeding carefully and thoughtfully in those weak areas may help

TIME FOR A TEST
1 Peter 1:7

THE POINT
Academic tests help us to understand what we know and don't know. Passing a test means our knowledge in a specific area of study is sufficient. Failing means we have work to do! Similarly, God's tests help us to realize where we are weak and where we are strong.

THE PREP
A few minutes to download a kids' trivia game onto an internet-connected device or to pull out a kids' trivia board game

THE PROPS
Kids' trivia game

THE PROCESS
- Download a kids' trivia game app, such as *Are You Smarter than a Fifth Grader?*, onto your smart-phone, Kindle, tablet, or other internet-connected device
- Ask trivia questions at the table and see how the kids do
- Talk about how trivia games, and tests, help us realize what we know and don't know
- Move on to discuss how God tests our obedience and knowledge from time to time. He doesn't need to see how we are doing because He knows already, but His tests help *us* see how we are doing!
- As a family, review how you have done with recent tests of patience, love, caring, hospitality, sharing, etc.
- Finish by praying and chatting about how each of you might do better the next time God gives a similar test

ATTITUDE AND OBEDIENCE
John 14:23 & 24

THE POINT
It is easy to obey authority when we like what we have been asked to do. It is not so easy to obey, however, when we do not like what we have been asked to do. Yet the test of real obedience is whether or not you follow through on the unpleasant tasks not the easy ones.

THE PREP
A few minutes to come up with some creative commands

THE PROPS
None

THE PROCESS
- Give your kids some "commands" that you know they will like, such as "eat another cookie," "go play video games for twenty-minutes," etc.
- After those "commands" have been obeyed, follow them up with instructions to do chores, or other things, that you know your children do *not* like
- When all your directives have been accomplished, discuss how it is much easier to obey when you like something than when you don't. However, the real test of obedience comes when you don't like something yet do it anyway—with a good attitude!
- Finish by isolating any areas where bad attitudes emerge and chat about how, in God's eyes, our attitudes matter as much as our actions in all areas of life—including obedience

RELEASING THE BURDEN
1 PETER 5:7

THE POINT
Many of us are loaded down with burdens. These burdens, however, are not ones that can be seen. Instead, they are invisible to the naked-eye, yet they are just as heavy as physical burdens. God never designed for us to carry such burdens, however. Instead, He desires that we release them over to Him.

THE PREP
Five to ten minutes to collect rocks or heavy items and load them into a durable book-bag or sack

THE PROPS
Heavy items such as rocks, bricks, books, weights, etc.; a book-bag or durable sack

THE PROCESS
- Load up a book-bag or sack with heavy items
- Have the kids put on the book-bag, or hold the sack, and go up and down the steps a couple times (as you stand near them so they don't fall)
- Take the book bag off and have them go up and down the steps again
- Ask which way was easier
- Discuss how we can choose to go through life carrying all of our problems, or we can give them all over to Jesus to carry for us
- Finish by talking about what burdens your family may need to turn over to the Lord

LIFE'S MAP
Proverbs 2:1-5

THE POINT
Arriving at a distant destination without GPS or a map is virtually impossible. Likewise, without the "map for life," aka the Bible, we won't make much spiritual progress either.

THE PREP
Five to ten minutes to hide some "treasure" and to create a "treasure map"

THE PROPS
An item you know your kids would like; a treasure map

THE PROCESS
- Hide something the kids would like (such as a bag of candy or a $5 bill) in a place that is virtually impossible to find
- Gather the kids and inform them that you have hidden a "treasure" somewhere in the house. Encourage them to search for it
- After some time has passed, and the kids are getting a bit frustrated, provide the map you have made to the location of the item
- Once the item is found, discuss with your kids how the Bible is like our map for life. As it was much easier to find the item with the map, so it is much easier to go through life when we consult God's map, the Bible, every day
- Finish by coming up with a plan to study God's map regularly as a family. I have several resources to do just that at www.markjmusser.com

GOT WISDOM?
Proverbs 3:5-7

THE POINT
Life is full of difficult choices, and we often don't know which way to turn. The Lord, however, has the wisdom and insight we need to make all the right choices. Our job is simply to seek His ways and rely on His guidance.

THE PREP
A few minutes to get a piece of paper, write "Problem Solved" on it, and affix it high on a wall

THE PROPS
Piece of paper; marker; tape or poster putty

THE PROCESS
- Affix a piece of paper to the wall that says, "Problem Solved!" Make sure the paper is well above the arm's reach of your tallest child
- Instruct your children to get the piece of paper without using any object to assist them
- After it proves impossible, offer to lift a child up to grab it
- Discuss how we cannot solve many of life's problems on our own. We need God to help us. When we ask Him, He gives us the strength and/or wisdom necessary to solve the problem or manage our way through it
- Finish by praying and asking the Lord to work in any situations going on in your family right now

GET PLUGGED IN
Ephesians 3:19 & 20

THE POINT
Many household items need a power source. Without a source of power, those items are completely useless. Likewise, without being plugged into the Lord, we will lack the power necessary to effectively make it through life.

THE PREP
A few minutes to choose a "loud item" that can be easily plugged in and unplugged

THE PROPS
A radio, TV, boom-box, or other "loud item"

THE PROCESS
- Plug in your "loud item," turn the volume up all the way, then hit the power button
- After an ear-splitting moment, unplug the device
- Discuss how that powerfully loud noise was instantly stopped by unplugging the device
- Move on to talk about how we have incredible power when we are plugged into God through Bible reading, prayer, devotions, etc. But we have *no* power when we are unplugged from Him
- Finish by formulating a family plan to make sure you are all *daily* plugged into the Lord

WALK THE TALK
Luke 6:46-49

THE POINT
Someone once said, "Your actions speak so loudly I can't hear what you are saying." That means that our actions carry weight, often even more weight than our words. Since that is the case, we must be ever vigilant to make sure our walk matches our talk.

THE PREP
None

THE PROPS
None

THE PROCESS
- Play a game of *Simon Says* with the children. Give them a command and follow that command with the corresponding action. For example, say, "Simon says touch your toes" and then touch your toes
- After playing the game that way for five or so rounds, switch the way you play (without informing your kids about the change)
- Begin to play so that your words and actions do *not* match. For example, say, "Simon Says touch your toes" but then touch your knees instead
- Do this several times with various body parts.
- After these "mismatches" cause some confusion (and possible complaints), discuss how it is important for our actions and words to match up. Otherwise, it can cause people to confuse what it means to be a Christian, which doesn't please God very much
- Finish by chatting about any areas in your family where the walk may not match the talk

WHAT WOULD YOU DO IF...
1 Corinthians 11:1; Ephesians 5:1 & 2

THE POINT
The word *Christian* means "Christ-one." That means those who consider themselves Christians should seek to emulate and imitate Christ in all situations. With that in mind, the question then becomes, "Well, how would Christ act in _____ situation?" As older Christians, we must help younger Christians answer such questions.

THE PREP
Five to ten minutes to add questions to the ones listed below

THE PROPS
A list of questions

THE PROCESS
- Go through some "What Would You Do If..." scenarios with the kids. See how they answer each one and provide feedback, correction, and/or praise as necessary
- What would you do if you were offered drugs?
- What would you do if a friend kept using curse words?
- What would you do if you were at a sleep-over and an inappropriate movie came on TV?
- What would you do if someone wanted to show you something bad on the internet?
- What would you do if you saw a classmate stealing something?
- What would you do if some of your friends were teasing someone?
- Feel free to come up with some of your own
- Make sure to help your kids know what Jesus would have them do in each situation
- Finish by asking the kids if they went through any recent situations and weren't sure how a Christian should respond

MIRRORS OF CHRIST
Philippians 3:17-20

THE POINT
The average non-Christian is *not* going to read the Bible or sit in church. Since that is the case, the only way such a person will see Christ is if we *show* him. With that in mind, we need to be asking ourselves, "When people listen to me speak, watch my actions, and observe my attitudes, do they see Christ?"

THE PREP
A few minutes to gather supplies and to practice writing "Look like Jesus" backwards, so it appears correctly in a mirror

THE PROPS
Washable marker. If you do not have a washable marker, a post-it note (or paper and tape) will suffice

THE PROCESS
- In washable marker write "Look like Jesus" backwards on your children's foreheads. (If you do not have a washable marker, use a post-it note or paper and tape)
- Have your children run to a mirror so they can tell what is written
- Discuss how they needed to look into a mirror to see what was written on their forehead
- Move on to talk about how people are looking at our lives to see how Christians should live, so we need to be careful that our choices and our life mirror Jesus' choices and life
- Finish by chatting about how well your family is doing at mirroring Jesus

READY TO OVERFLOW
Psalm 63:1-5

THE POINT
An old Chinese proverb states that whatever we are filled with comes out when we are bumped. The average person can "act nice" when things are going well. But once "the bumps of life" come along, we can really see what is inside of a person. This is why it is important to be filled with the Lord and His Word. When the tough times come, we want Him flowing from us.

THE PREP
A few minutes to gather supplies and prepare a glass of water

THE PROPS
A clear glass; water; twenty or so pennies

THE PROCESS
- Fill a clear glass with water so that the surface of the water is even with the very top of the glass
- Make sure the top of the glass is no higher than your child's eye-level
- Start sliding pennies down the inside of the glass. (Do not "plop" them in. Make sure to carefully slide each down the inside of the glass)
- Watch as the water level actually rises above the edge of the glass without spilling over
- Eventually, as you carefully add more coins, the water will begin to spill over
- When that happens, explain that when something is full, it will eventually begin to spill out. Likewise, if we are full of God's love, that love should be spilling out to others
- Finish by discussing what usually flows from your family when "the bumps of life" occur. Talk about any changes that may need to be made

GOD'S KINGDOM FIRST, MINE SECOND
Matthew 6:31-33

THE POINT
A line from the song "In the Blink of Eye," by Mercy Me, states, "How can I further Your kingdom when I'm so wrapped up in mine." In other words, I cannot build God's kingdom when I have made my own kingdom the priority. As Christians, we must always guard against mistaking whose kingdom matters in the end.

THE PREP
A few minutes to prepare some videos

THE PROPS
The two video links below

THE PROCESS
- Discuss how children and teens CAN make a difference no matter how young. (See videos)
- Talk to your children, and pray about, what they and you can do to be difference makers for Jesus
- Cut TV and video game time in half for the next week or so. Use that extra time to invest in a ministry
- After that time is up, you just may find that your family is better off with *less* TV/video game time and *more* service!

VIDEO LINKS
- https://www.youtube.com/watch?v=b3_V84gbUZs
- https://www.youtube.com/watch?v=71wTZzwfG0M

CONTROLLED BY LOVE
John 13:34 & 35

THE POINT
Over a dozen times in the New Testament, Christians are commanded to love one another. Such a command is central to the Christian life. After all, Jesus Himself stated, "Your love for one another will prove to the world that you are My disciples" (John 13:35).

THE PREP
A couple minutes to gather supplies

THE PROPS
Blank paper; crayons or markers

THE PROCESS
- Give the kids blank pieces of paper
- Have them draw a big heart on it and write "Jesus Loves You" in the middle of the heart
- Allow them to color in the heart if they wish
- Instruct the kids to give that heart to someone *outside* of the family this week
- Discuss why it is so important to show Jesus' love to everyone
- Brainstorm ways your family can do that on a regular basis

TIME TO TRANSFORM
2 Corinthians 5:15

THE POINT
Christ did not live, die, and rise again so that we could be "slightly improved." No, His death and resurrection allows us to be completely cleansed of sin and totally transformed into a new creation!

THE PREP
Five to ten minutes to download items and gather supplies

THE PROPS
Pictures of a caterpillar and of a butterfly; crayons, markers, or different colored pens

THE PROCESS
- Print out a picture of a caterpillar
- Print out a picture of a butterfly
- Show the kids the picture of the caterpillar you printed and explain that you are now going to make this caterpillar brand new
- Proceed to recolor it with a marker, pen, crayon, or colored pencil
- Ask your children if you really just made this caterpillar new
- Next, show the picture of the butterfly and explain that it is actually the new "caterpillar"
- Explain how when we accept Jesus, He doesn't just want to make us "a little better." Instead, He wants to *completely* change us from the inside out
- Finish by discussing things in your family that may need Jesus' transformative touch

LETTING GOD TAKE OVER
Galatians 2:19 & 20

THE POINT
One of the biggest keys to the Christian life is giving up control. Each of us must hand over the controls of our lives to the Creator, trusting that He is infinitely more able than us to guide our lives.

THE PREP
A few minutes to find (A) a remote control vehicle or (B) to gather supplies

THE PROPS
(A) Blindfold; a remote control vehicle; (B) book; blank paper; colored pencil or crayon

THE PROCESS (A)
- If you have a remote control vehicle, put a blindfold on a child and have him or her work to control this vehicle without being able to see
- Next, take the blindfold off and have your child control the vehicle being able to see everything
- Discuss how we don't know as much as God does. He can see everything—even the future. We need to give Him control because He can do a better job at "directing" our lives
- Finish by chatting about what areas of your family members' lives have not been given over to the Lord yet

THE PROCESS (B)
- If you do not have a remote control vehicle, try this instead
- Have your child place a book on his or her head then place a piece of blank paper on top of the book. (The book simply is used to create a drawing surface)
- Hand your child a crayon, pen, or marker and have him or her draw a Christmas tree with candy canes *on* the tree and presents *under* the tree
- After your child is finished, let him or her see the finished product

- Now allow your child to draw the same thing again—this time the "regular way"
- Go on to discuss what was mentioned above

FRUIT INSPECTION
Matthew 7:15-20

THE POINT
Just as you can identify trees by the fruit, flowers, or leaves they produce, so others are able to identify us by the kind of "fruit" produced through our lives. If you cannot be readily identified as a Christian by others, then perhaps some "fruit inspection" is necessary.

THE PREP
Five to ten minutes to gather fruit or supplies

THE PROPS
Blindfold; pieces of various fruit; if not readily available, other items that can be identified by touch and smell like a shoe, candle, toothpaste, peanut butter, etc.

THE PROCESS
- Blindfold your child and hand him or her various pieces of fruit. Allow your child to feel and smell the pieces, then guess what each piece is
- If you do not have fruit in the home, use other items that can be identified by touch and/or smell (see list above)
- After the blindfold comes off, discuss how your child was able to identify each item by its distinctive characteristics. Likewise, people should be able to identify your family as Christian by your distinctive lifestyle
- Talk about ways you are doing well at this and also what areas may need improvement

WHATCHA THINKIN' ABOUT?
Colossians 3:1-4

THE POINT
A simple character-formation formula goes like this: Sow a thought, reap an action. Sow an action, reap a habit. Sow a habit, and reap your character. This formula shows that our characters are formed first by what we choose to think about and dwell on. With that being the case, how important is it for us to spend time dwelling on the things of Heaven.

THE PREP
Five to ten minutes writing or typing out some words and phrases

THE PROPS
Ten to twelve sheets of paper; printer or pen/Sharpie

THE PROCESS
- Write out, or print out, a bunch of words and phrases on separate pieces of paper
- Some of the words should represent "the things of Heaven," such as *Jesus, the Bible, cross, church, serving others, prayer, loving others*, etc.
- Other words should represent "the things of earth," such as listing a favorite sports' team, famous actor, latest song, favorite game, friends, fun activities, etc.
- Gather all these words and phrases into a pile and tell your kids that they need to identify each word or phrase as a "thing of Heaven" or a "thing of earth"
- After you go through them all, remind your family that Colossians 3 says to not just think about the things of earth but also to focus on the things of Heaven
- Discuss how your family will draw closer to Jesus and learn to become more like Him as you all focus on His things and not just earth's things

GET CONNECTED
John 15:1-8

THE POINT
Jesus says that apart from Him we can do nothing (John 15:5), yet how often do we try to do things our own way? This is not how the Christian life is meant to be lived. We are to stay dependent and connected to the Lord at all times.

THE PREP
A minute or less

THE PROPS
An unplugged TV

THE PROCESS
- Unplug your TV
- Sometime during the day, tell your family you'd like to sit down together to watch a TV show or play a video game
- As you go to do so, ask a child to turn the TV on
- When it doesn't come on, see if your child can figure out the problem
- After the problem has been discovered, discuss how the TV can't really do anything without being connected to a power source. Likewise, we need to be daily connected to God to do great things
- Talk about things your family can do to stay connected the Lord
- Finish by coming up with a game plan to stay connected on a *daily* basis

WASHED CLEAN
1 John 1:8 & 9

THE POINT
The Bible is clear: All of us have sinned and fallen short of the glory of God (Romans 3:23). Thankfully, that is not the end of the story. Though dirtied by sin, we can be forgiven of our sins and made clean through Christ's death and resurrection!

THE PREP
A couple minutes to gather supplies

THE PROPS
Washable markers; soap and water

THE PROCESS
- Talk to your child about different kinds of sin—have him or her give examples of ways to sin by speaking, by doing, and by thinking
- As your child gives examples, write each one down on his or her arms. Soon your child's arms will be covered "in sin"
- Discuss how we all do, say, and think many bad things and it covers us with sin. But when we ask Jesus for forgiveness, He comes and cleanses (washes) our sin away, leaving NO trace
- Take your child to the kitchen sink or tub and wash away "the sin"
- Talk about how we don't need to be continually embarrassed or ashamed of what we did in the past. If we asked for forgiveness, no trace is left. It is gone!
- Finish by giving your family a chance to pray and seek forgiveness for any sin anyone may have committed

BEING MADE NEW
1 Timothy 1:14-16

THE POINT
Because sin has distorted and marred us, we are not as God originally created us to be. But praise the Lord, through Christ we can be remade and restored!

THE PREP
A few minutes of research

THE PROPS
Before and after pictures of restored furniture, cars, houses, or other items

THE PROCESS
- Go to Pinterest or a web-browsing site and seek out furniture, car, and/or home restoration before and after pictures
- Show your child the before and after pictures and talk about the amount of time and loving care that goes into restoring items so that they can look brand new
- Go on to discuss how God does the same thing with us. Sin mars us, hurts us, scratches and scuffs us up, but God wants to come along and go to work—healing us, forgiving us, and making us brand new again!
- Spend some time praying, asking God to do His restoring work in your family

KINGDOM HEIRS
Galatians 4:4-7

THE POINT
When we accept Christ, we are adopted by God—the King of Kings and Lord of Lords. As children of God, we are now heirs to the Kingdom of Heaven. All of its riches and privileges belong to us. Further, all of the responsibilities are ours as well.

THE PREP
Ten minutes to gather supplies and do some research

THE PROPS
Construction paper; tape; crayons or markers; scissors; research on etiquette for English royalty

THE PROCESS
- Have several pieces of construction paper (or blank paper) handy and have the kids make crowns (You may need to tape two pieces of paper together for those with larger heads)
- As you and the children talk about how a child of the King of Kings should live, have the kids decorate, color, and cut out their crowns
- Have the kids practice some of the requirements of English royalty—the bow, the curtsy, the proper holding of the tea cup, etc.
- You may even want to have dinner "as royalty." Have the kids dress up, speak in "high language," drink with the pinky extended, napkins on the lap, etc.
- Finish by discussing ways your family can practice the requirements of Heavenly royalty—loving others, serving others, honoring God, being thankful, etc.

TIME IN THE WORD
2 Timothy 3:16 & 17

THE POINT
Next to salvation through Jesus, the Bible is God's greatest gift to humanity. Being in His Word on a regular basis is literally life-changing because it is filled with wisdom, insight, direction, inspiration, correction, and hope.

THE PREP
Roughly 15 minutes

THE PROPS
Two eggs—one of them hard-boiled; *Sharpie* or permanent marker

THE PROCESS
- Have two eggs—one hard boiled and the other not
- With *Sharpie* or marker write "Good" on the hard-boiled egg, while on the regular egg write "Bad"
- Spin the hard-boiled egg. It should spin well, almost like a top
- Spin the regular egg. It will not spin as well or as long
- Discuss how the hard-boiled egg spent a good bit of time in boiling water and the other egg did not. Because the hard-boiled one spent that time in hot water, it did a lot better
- Note that, likewise, as we spend time with God and His Word, we can do a lot better at life. We can have more peace, hope, direction, wisdom, etc.
- Without spending time with God and His Word, we don't have the same peace, hope, direction, wisdom, etc.
- Finish by talking about how your family can spend time in God's Word regularly.

TREASURE SEEKER
Matthew 13:44-46

THE POINT
"You get as much out of something as you put into it." This saying is certainly true, and especially so when it comes to the Kingdom of Heaven. If you want to get *all* that God has for you, then you must be willing to give *all* of yourself to get it!

THE PREP
Five to ten minutes to prepare a treasure hunt

THE PROPS
A "treasure" such as a bag of candy or some money; four to six quarters (or other change); clue sheets equal to the amount of quarters you choose; papers that say, "Give a quarter for the next clue."

THE PROCESS
- Hide something your children will really like, such as a bag of candy or a few dollars
- Be prepared to distribute around four to six quarters between your children. For example, if you have two children, you can give them each two quarters
- Prepare clues equal to the amount of quarters you distribute. For example, if you have given out four quarters, prepare four clues
- Tell your children that you have hidden something fantastic in the house. To find it, however, they will need clues. And each clue will cost a quarter
- Have your children give you one quarter to get the first clue. After they discover the location of the next clue, have them give you a quarter for the following clue, and so on
- In the end, they will need to give up *all* their quarters to get the "treasure"

EXAMPLE
- One way to do this is as follows: Get the quarter for the first clue which can say something like: "Go to where we keep our towels." Your kids will

wander to the towel closet. In that closet, you will have placed a paper which says, "Give Dad a quarter to get the next clue." That clue can read: "How many cans of soup do we have? Go and find out." When your kids get to where you keep the soup, on top of one of the cans can be the next paper which says, "Give Dad a quarter to get the next clue"
- Have enough clues for each quarter. The last clue, then, will lead to the "treasure"
- Go on to discuss with your children how they needed to give up *all* their quarters to get the treasure, and God wants us to be willing to give up everything to have His treasure—eternal life in Heaven
- Finish by talking about where your family can sacrifice time, talent, and money to serve the Lord and build His kingdom

ALIEN INVASION
1 Peter 2:11 & 12

THE POINT
1 Peter 2:11 states that we are "aliens" here on earth. We do not belong here because our citizenship is in Heaven. Since that is case, we should not be living as if earth is our home. Our actions, the words we use, the thoughts we think, and the way we spend our free-time should be different from those who do not claim citizenship in Heaven.

THE PREP
A few minutes with Google Translator

THE PROPS
Internet connection; paper and pen to write down some information

THE PROCESS
- Go to google translator and type in the phrase "My name is _____, and I am a Christian" for multiple languages
- Copy that phrase down in each language you choose and share them with your kids
- Discuss with your kids how the word "alien" in 1 Peter 2:11 literally means "foreigner" or "from another place," then ask how they could tell the words you were using weren't from America (or whatever country you live in)
- Go on to discuss how it is usually easy to tell if people are "aliens" (foreigners) because they talk differently and usually act differently as well
- Similarly, as Christians, who belong to Heaven, we should talk and act differently from those who are not Christians
- Visual cues are also great reminders. Consider purchasing an alien stuffed animal as a reminder to your kids that you are foreigners here on earth.
- Finish by evaluating if your family looks and acts more like the neighbors or more like Jesus

STICKING OUT IN A CROWD
Philippians 1:27

THE POINT
Living a Christian lifestyle should cause us to stick out. However, many Christians work harder at blending into the world around them than sticking out for Christ.

THE PREP
A few minutes of internet searching

THE PROPS
Internet connection; printed pictures

THE PROCESS
- Go to an image search engine like *Google* or *Bing* and type in "sticking out in a crowd"
- Choose a few pictures to print out or display for your kids that show items quite clearly sticking out
- Next type in "Where's Waldo" and choose a picture or two to display. It would be best to choose ones that make it very difficult to find Waldo
- Show the first set of pictures and have the kids choose the item or color that is clearly sticking out
- Next, pull out the "Where's Waldo" pictures and have your kids attempt to find Waldo
- It should prove *much more* difficult to find Waldo than it did to find the items that stuck out in the previous set of pictures
- Take time to discuss if your family is more like Waldo or more like the other items
- Do you all clearly stick out as Christians, or do you tend to blend in with the world around you?

STOP THE CONFUSION
Ezekiel 36:20-22

THE POINT
As Christians, we bear the name of Christ. Bearing this great name is both an honor and a responsibility. When we live as Christ would live, people can see Him and honor comes to His name. When we do not, people do not see Christ. They become confused as to whom Christ really is, and God is not honored.

THE PREP
A few minutes to prepare a space for a game

THE PROPS
A rectangular open space about ten feet by five feet; string or masking tape to divide the space into three equal sections

THE PROCESS
- Play a game of "Vanilla, Chocolate, Strawberry" with the kids
- To play, create a rectangular space on the floor and divide it into three equal sections big enough for everyone who is playing to stand in
- Call one of the end spaces "Vanilla," call the middle space "Chocolate," and call the remaining space "Strawberry"
- Have everyone start in the middle (Chocolate) and explain the rules
- You will call out one word--either "Vanilla," "Chocolate," or "Strawberry." Once you call it out, everyone must go to that space
- If someone goes to the wrong space, he is out. If you call the space everyone is in and someone leaves that space, he is out. Finally, if you are playing with multiple people, the last person into the called space is out
- Start playing by calling out a space and have everyone move into it. You may even choose to point to that space for emphasis (and also help set up what comes next)
- After doing that for a bit, begin to call out a space but point to a space other than the one you chose. For example, call out "Vanilla" but point to "Chocolate"
- Continue doing that for five or six calls
- Afterwards, discuss which was easier to follow: you calling the spot and

- pointing to it, or you calling the spot and pointing to another
- Move on to talk about how, as Christians, when our words and actions don't line up, it creates confusion
- As Christians we need to make sure our words and actions line up, so no one is confused about what a Christian should be like
- Finish by chatting about how your family is doing at "living like Jesus"

HEY, WHAT'S THAT SMELL?
2 Corinthians 2:14 & 15

THE POINT
We have all entered a house and smelled cookies or brownies baking. Such a smell draws us into the kitchen rather quickly. Conversely, we have also entered rooms or buildings that didn't quite smell so good. Such odors usually sent us running! Similarly, our actions also emit a fragrance that will either draw people to Christ or push them away.

THE PREP
The time it takes to bake or microwave something with a pleasant aroma

THE PROPS
A sweet-smelling food to bake such as cookies or brownies, or something to microwave like a bag of buttered popcorn

THE PROCESS
- Sometime during the day, bake something with a distinctive aroma like cookies or brownies. (If you do not have the time or the materials to bake, a bag of microwave popcorn is a good substitute)
- It is quite possible your kids will notice the smell of what you are baking (or microwaving) even before you bring up what is written below
- Talk about how noticeable the smell is, how it fills the house, and how you can instantly tell what the food is just by that distinctive smell
- Go on to discuss how we, as Christians, should be noticeably and distinctively like Christ, so much so that people who don't even know we are Christians can tell there is something different about us
- Finish by chatting about how your family's words and actions are impacting the world around them—neighbors, classmates, friends, teammates, etc.

DULL OR BRIGHT
2 Corinthians 3:7 & 8

THE POINT
In Matthew 5, Jesus calls us to be lights that shine brightly for Him. We accomplish this as we seek to speak and act and live like Christ. When we do those things well, our lives shine brightly. When we fail, the bulb gets quite dim.

THE PREP
A couple minutes to gather supplies and prepare

THE PROPS
Two flashlights; tape; a dark room

WHAT ABOUT IT?
- Grab two flashlights. Cover the "bright end" of one with duct tape or something similar
- Take the kids into a dark room with both flashlights and ask, "To get some light in this room, which flashlight should we use?"
- Smart-alecks aside, the kids will choose the one that actually creates a strong beam of light
- While still in the room, discuss that our world is a dark place, but Jesus has called us to be a light
- He needs us to live in such a way that we shine out brightly for Him, not block His light by our attitudes, actions, etc.
- Finish by discussing how your family can shine brightly for Jesus

STUCK IN THE SOIL
1 John 2:24 & 25

THE POINT
As we strive to stay connected to the Lord through Bible study, prayer, and church; our spiritual lives can thrive and our hearts feel full. Neglecting the things that keep us connected to Christ, however, cause us to whither. Without that life-giving connection, our lives are not nearly as full and satisfying.

THE PREP
Initially, a few minutes to gather supplies and prepare; another couple days to wait for decay

THE PROPS
Flowers or grass in soil; flowers or grass out of soil

THE PROCESS
- If you have flowers, take one out of the soil while leaving the rest in the soil. If you do not have flowers, you can dig up a small section of grass (keeping the roots in the soil) and then pull out one or two blades of grass while allowing the rest to stay in the soil
- Compare the flowers in the soil (or blades of grass) with those not in the soil over the next few days
- After the difference starts to become very clear, discuss how, at first, there didn't appear to be much of a difference. However, as time passed, it became very easy to distinguish between the ones connected to the soil and the ones *not* connected
- Likewise, when we start to neglect the things that keep us connected to Jesus, it may not be noticeable at first. However, the longer we neglect those things, the easier it is to tell that we are "disconnected"
- Finish by talking about how well your family is staying connected to the Lord

ALWAYS BEST TO OBEY
John 14:15

THE POINT
There is a constant battle going on all around us. On one hand you have Christ calling us to obedience, while on the other hand you have Satan working to lead us astray. Because of this, in order to best follow Christ, we must constantly be on guard and watching out for Satan's tricks.

THE PREP
A few minutes to create some commands

THE PROPS
Ten to twelve pieces of paper; *Sharpie* or marker

THE PROCESS
- Play a variation of *Simon Says*, which we will call *Jesus Says vs. Satan Says*
- Prepare ten to twelve pieces of paper with commands, written in the center of each page, that say things like: "touch your knees," "tap your head," "clap your hands"
- At the top of half of these sheets, write "Jesus Says." On the top of the other half, write "Satan Says" (If you are playing with some young ones who cannot read, use a cross symbol for "Jesus Says" and a pitchfork for "Satan Says")
- As you play the game, say the command at the center of the page, but do *not* say whether Jesus or Satan says
- Your children will need to pay attention not only to your voice, but also to the words (or symbol) on the page
- They should only do the commands labeled "Jesus Says." Anyone caught doing what "Satan Says" is out
- After you have gone through all the papers, discuss with your children how, to be successful at the game, they needed to pause a moment and think about if it was Jesus or Satan saying it

- Likewise, obeying Jesus isn't always easy because Satan will try to trick us. So we need to be careful to pause and think before we make choices in order to best obey Jesus
- Finish by discussing ways to do just that

MULTIPLYING THE KINGDOM
Romans 10:13-15

THE POINT
One person can make a BIG difference. If you lead two people to the Lord, and they each lead two people to the Lord, and they each lead two people to the Lord, and they each lead two people to the Lord, pretty soon the numbers of new believers are sky-rocketing!

THE PREP
A few minutes to gather candy or coins

THE PROPS
128 pieces of candy or 128 coins

THE PROCESS
- Have 128 pieces of candy ready (M&M's, Skittles, Hershey Kisses, etc.). If you do not have candy, you can use 128 pennies (or other coins)
- Pull out one piece and explain that this piece represents one person who goes and tells someone about Jesus
- Pull out a second piece and share that there are now two people who believe in Jesus, and they both go out and each tells another person
- Grab two more pieces so that you have four. Continue by letting your children know that these four went off and each told another person about Jesus
- Pull four more pieces out so that you have eight. Keep doing this through 16, 32, and then 64
- When you get to 64, say they all went out and told another person about Jesus. Dump out the rest of the pieces and say, "Now 128 people believe in Jesus and will be in Heaven."
- Go on to discuss with your family how those 128 all started with just one person who told another person about Jesus
- Talk about how your family can tell others about Jesus

THE RUB OFF
1 Corinthians 15:33

THE POINT
Whoever, or whatever, you spend time with will rub off on you. If you spend time with bad influences, you will find yourself moving further from the Lord. Conversely, if you spend time with those who love the Lord, you will find yourself drawing closer to Him.

THE PREP
A few minutes to gather supplies

THE PROPS
Blank paper; graphite pencils

THE PROCESS
- Give each child a blank piece of paper and a pencil
- Have them press down hard with the pencil and write the words "FRIENDS" in big, thick, and dark letters (those instructions will be important for the next step)
- After they have done so, have them rub their fingers across the letters. This should cause them to have considerable graphite residue on their fingertips
- Talk about how spending time with people causes them to rub off on you. You might mention some examples from your family—how you use similar phrases, say the same things when frustrated, etc.
- Continue by noting that, similarly, when we spend time with God, we give the Lord a chance to rub off on us
- That means the more time we spend with God, the more we will become like Him
- Finish by talking about how your family can do just that

CHANGING YOUR MIND
Philippians 2:4 & 5

THE POINT
The focus of our thoughts is often the focus of our lives. If you spend a great deal of time focused on self and worldly pursuits, your life will reflect that. Conversely, if you focus on the Lord and Heavenly pursuits, your life will reflect that.

THE PREP
A few minutes to gather some pictures

THE PROPS
Two pictures—each one of a different animal

PROCESS
- Print out, or display, two pictures—each of a different animal, then prepare to "test" your kids
- Show them the picture of one of the animals and tell them to stare at it intently for twenty seconds. When that time is up, have them close their eyes, then ask what they are thinking about while their eyes are shut
- Do the same with another animal
- Often, our thoughts revolve around what we were just focusing on. Use this to discuss how when we focus on ourselves, our thoughts usually center on "Me-Me," but if we spend time focusing on Jesus, our thoughts will change as well and we will be less self-centered and more kingdom centered
- Finish by talking about what your family can do to keep a focus on Jesus and His kingdom

PICKED BACK UP
Psalm 147:1-3

THE POINT
We humans are a sinful, fallen bunch. We constantly make mistakes—sometimes the same mistakes over and over again. Thankfully, we serve a God who is full of grace and goodness. Each time we fall, we can turn to the Lord and be pulled back up to our feet.

THE PREP
A few minutes to set up dominos

THE PROPS
Dominos or other items that can be easily lined up and toppled over

THE PROCESS
- Set up a series of ten to twelve dominos. (If you do not have dominos, you can use *Lego* pieces, *Scrabble* tiles, or even hard cover books)
- Gather your kids around what you have set up and talk about how you carefully arranged these dominos (or what you used) just exactly as you want them to be. Yet, one thing can ruin it all
- Tip over the first domino and watch as they all fall over
- Discuss how life is like that. We want things to be perfect, and we work to make it that way, but our sin and life's problems can ruin everything quite quickly
- Set everything back up and, as you do, explain that this is what Jesus does. He takes our imperfect lives that are messed up, and He helps make everything all right again
- And when things fall apart all over again, He is right there to help pick back up the pieces that time as well

EPILOGUE

I hope God has truly blessed your family (or class) as you used this book. I know He deeply desires to do so many awesome things in and through you. His plan for your children is truly remarkable! I trust you have grabbed hold of that.

If you have been blessed in any way through these object lessons, please do me the great favor of leaving a positive review on Amazon. Your review just may encourage another family to take this same journey.

Be sure to check my website www.markjmusser.com

GOD BLESS YOU!

Made in the USA
Coppell, TX
18 November 2019